CAUSES OF WORLD WAR I

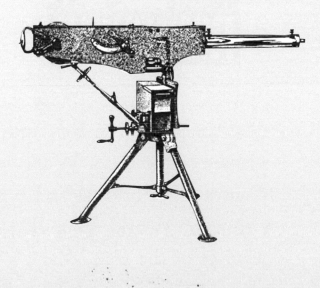

ROAD TO WAR
CAUSES OF CONFLICT

Causes of the American Revolution
Causes of the Civil War
Causes of World War I
Causes of World War II
Causes of the Iraq War

ROAD TO WAR
CAUSES OF CONFLICT

CAUSES OF WORLD WAR I

John Ziff

OTTN
PUBLISHING
STOCKTON, NJ

OTTN Publishing
16 Risler Street
Stockton, NJ 08859
www.ottnpublishing.com

First printing

3 5 7 9 8 6 4 2

Library of Congress Cataloging-in-Publication Data

Ziff, John.
  Causes of World War I / John Ziff.
     p. cm. — (The road to war)
  Summary: "Describes the causes of World War I, including compe-
tition between Europe's Great Powers for economic and political
dominance, instability in the Balkan Peninsula, and the assassination
of the heir to the Austro-Hungarian throne"—Provided by publisher.
  Includes bibliographical references and index.
  ISBN-13: 978-1-59556-003-2 (hardcover)
  ISBN-10: 1-59556-003-3 (hardcover)
  ISBN-13: 978-1-59556-007-0 (pbk.)
  ISBN-10: 1-59556-007-6 (pbk.)
  1. World War, 1914-1918—Causes. I. Title: Causes of World War
1. II. Title: Causes of World War One. III. Title. IV. Series.
  D511.Z554 2005
  940.3'11—dc22
                                          2005015103

**Frontispiece: German cavalry soldiers parade through Berlin on their
way to the front, August 1914. In the German capital, as elsewhere in
Europe, the outbreak of World War I was greeted with considerable
enthusiasm.**

TABLE OF CONTENTS

Notable Figures 6

1   Incident in Sarajevo............9

2   European Harmony:
     The Great Illusion 17

3   Rivals for Power 29

4   July 1914 45

5   The Great War..................61

Chronology 66

Glossary 68

Further Reading......................69

Internet Resources.................70

Index......................................71

NOTABLE FIGURES

BERCHTOLD, LEOPOLD VON (1863–1942). Berchtold believed that Serbia presented a grave threat to the survival of Austria-Hungary, which he served as foreign minister.

BETHMANN-HOLLWEG, THEOBALD VON (1856–1921). The German chancellor is believed to have formulated the abortive plan by which Austria would defeat Serbia before Europe's Great Powers had a chance to intervene.

BISMARCK, OTTO VON (1815–1898). One of Europe's ablest statesmen, he masterminded the unification of Germany and thereafter guided its foreign policy for nearly two decades as chancellor.

CONRAD VON HÖTZENDORF, FRANZ (1852–1925). The chief of staff of the Austrian army, he delayed attacking Serbia after the assassination of Franz Ferdinand, thereby making it much more likely that a general European war would occur.

FRANZ FERDINAND (1863–1914). The archduke, heir to the throne of Austria-Hungary, was assassinated in Sarajevo.

GREY, SIR EDWARD (1862–1933). Britain's foreign secretary, Grey made various proposals to avoid war during July of 1914 but pushed strongly for Britain's entry on the side of France and Russia after Germany violated Belgium's neutrality.

JAGOW, GOTTLIEB VON (1863–1935). Germany's foreign minister, he formulated the unsuccessful strategy

| Theobald von Bethmann-Hollweg | Franz Ferdinand | Kaiser Wilhelm |

of localizing the conflict between Austria and Serbia; later he undermined the peacemaking efforts of Kaiser Wilhelm.

MOLTKE, HELMUTH JOHANNES LUDWIG VON (1848–1916). As head of the German General Staff, Moltke advocated a preventive war against Russia and France, and he undercut the kaiser's last-minute efforts to avert a European conflict.

NICHOLAS II (1868–1918). The czar of Russia, he tried unsuccessfully to work with his cousin, Kaiser Wilhelm II, to avoid war during the final days of July 1914.

POINCARÉ, RAYMOND (1860–1934). In the years leading up to World War I, Poincaré, president of France from 1913 to 1920, advocated close ties with Russia and Britain but was not considered anti-German.

PRINCIP, GAVRILO (1894?–1918). A Bosnian Serb nationalist, he assassinated Franz Ferdinand in Sarajevo.

TISZA, ISTVÁN (1861–1918). The prime minister of Hungary opposed a quick strike against Serbia following the assassination of Franz Ferdinand.

WILHELM II (1859–1941). After becoming kaiser in 1888, Wilhelm steered Germany on an erratic course that frequently heightened international tensions; his efforts to resolve the war crisis of 1914 were undermined by German generals and government officials.

INCIDENT IN SARAJEVO

Franz Ferdinand and his wife, Sophie, sit in the backseat of the motorcar that will take them through the streets of Sarajevo, June 28, 1914. Among the throngs of people lining the archduke's parade route was Bosnian Serb nationalist Gavrilo Princip (bottom left), the leader of a plot to assassinate the heir to the Austro-Hungarian throne.

O n a June morning more than 90 years ago, five men and a woman climbed into an open motorcar for a short ride through the streets of Sarajevo. Before the automobile set out, a photographer snapped a picture. He could not have known that within a few minutes, two of the people in his photo would be dead.

This was a time when emperors and kings still ruled many areas—and, in fact, the man in the backseat of the motorcar in the photo was *heir* to an important throne. Archduke Franz Ferdinand would become the ruler of Austria-Hungary upon the death of his aged uncle, Emperor Franz Joseph, who was then in the 66th year of his reign.

Austria-Hungary—also known as the Dual Monarchy—stretched across some 260,000 square miles in

Austria-Hungary's southernmost province, Bosnia-Herzegovina, was a hotbed of Slavic nationalist agitation. Some of it was encouraged by people in neighboring Serbia.

central Europe. Within the borders of this Texas-sized realm lived approximately 50 million people. They came from nearly a dozen national groups, each speaking its own language and retaining its own customs. The most important of these peoples were the Germans, the Magyars, and the *Slavs*.

Politically, Germans dominated Austria-Hungary's ethnic hodgepodge, but they constituted less than one-quarter of its total population. And that made governing difficult. Emperor Franz Joseph had earlier found it necessary to grant special political rights to his Magyar subjects, but *nationalism* still simmered among other ethnic groups who resented being ruled by the German-speaking Austrians. Some members of these groups believed they deserved their own state. Nowhere was this attitude stronger than in the *Balkans*, at the southernmost extent of Austria-Hungary's territory. Here, in the province of Bosnia-Herzegovina, home to Slavic peoples such as Serbs and Croats, only the presence of several hundred thousand Austrian soldiers kept a lid on nationalist tensions.

It was for the purpose of observing the army's annual maneuvers that Franz Ferdinand journeyed from the Austrian capital of Vienna to Bosnia in June 1914. The archduke had decided to combine his official duties with a weekend holiday, bringing his wife,

Sophie, along with him. She can be seen next to Franz Ferdinand, wearing a white dress and shading her face with a parasol, in the photograph taken before their motorcade started out on its drive through the Bosnian town of Sarajevo. The trace of a smile seems to play across Sophie's face, and we must assume she was happy: this day, June 28, was her wedding anniversary.

CONSPIRACY

For seven young men in the crowd lining the route of the archduke's motorcade, June 28 was also a date laden with meaning. On that date in 1389, a Turkish army had defeated Serb forces at the Battle of Kosovo. Ethnic Serbs considered this the end of the medieval kingdom of Serbia, which had controlled much of the Balkan Peninsula. What followed was centuries of rule—and, Serbs believed, repression— by the Ottoman Turks.

The Balkans weren't the only region conquered by the Turkish Ottoman Empire, however. At its height, the empire, whose beginnings date to about 1300, controlled Anatolia (the part of modern-day Turkey that lies within Asia), a large swath of territory in northern Africa, much of the Middle East, the Caucasus region and part of southern Russia, and Europe as far north and west as Hungary. In 1529, the armies of the Ottoman sultan even reached the gates of Vienna, and it appeared that the Muslim Turks might overrun all of Christian Europe.

That did not happen, and from the 17th century on, the Ottoman Empire suffered a long decline. Corruption and governmental incompetence ate away at the empire from within, while countries that the Turks had earlier menaced—including Russia and Austria—pressed on it relentlessly from without. By the mid-1800s, the other major European powers scorned the Ottoman Empire as "the Sick Man of Europe."

In 1878, after enduring a military defeat at the hands of Russia, the Ottomans were essentially forced out of the Balkans by a settlement that the European powers imposed at the Congress of Berlin. The congress decided to recognize Serbia and Montenegro as independent states. Bosnia and Herzegovina were to remain part of the Ottoman sultan's realm in name, but Austria-Hungary was given actual authority to administer the twin provinces.

Not everyone was pleased by this settlement. Some in the newly independent Serbia believed that their country should include more territory, including Bosnia and Herzegovina, which they considered a part of historical Serbia. Some ethnic Serbs in Bosnia and Herzegovina agreed, while others simply resented the Austrian military occupation. Intrigues and plots were hatched, and broken up, frequently.

The situation became more volatile after 1908, when officials in Vienna decided to *annex* Bosnia and Herzegovina. In response, a secret group known as the Black Hand was formed. Its members, who included officers in the Serbian army, were extreme nationalists dedicated to unifying all the lands where Serbs lived by whatever means necessary.

On the morning of June 28, 1914, as Franz Ferdinand's motorcar made its way toward the Sarajevo city hall, seven young Bosnians in the crowd clutched weapons they had received from a Black Hand officer. Their mission: to kill the archduke.

At a bridge, one of the conspirators, Nedjelko Cabrinovic, stepped forward and hurled a bomb. But it sailed over the archduke's motorcar, exploding in the street. Fragments injured about a dozen spectators, as well as several people in the car that followed Franz Ferdinand's. Because the crowd was so large and noisy, however, few people heard the explosion or realized that anything out of the ordinary had taken place. The motorcade proceeded toward the city hall, passing other conspirators, but none of them made a move. It appeared that the assassination attempt would fail.

Upon arriving at city hall, the archduke listened to a welcoming speech by Sarajevo's mayor, then delivered a few brief remarks of his own. After the ceremony, he insisted on going to the hospital to visit the people who had been wounded in the bomb attack. On the way, the driver of the lead car took a wrong turn and, realizing his mistake, braked to turn around. As fate would have it, Franz Ferdinand's car stopped directly in front of the leader of the Bosnian Serb conspirators, Gavrilo Princip. The youth stepped forward, pulled out his revolver, and fired twice, hitting Sophie in the stomach and Franz Ferdinand in the neck. Both died quickly.

The assassinations set in motion a chain of events that would result in the bloodiest conflict the world had ever seen: the First World War. By the time this conflict ended in November 1918, more than 40 million people had died or been wounded. Yet the murders in Sarajevo, by themselves, did not cause World War I to begin, as is sometimes assumed. Many factors were at work in the outbreak of the fighting during the summer of 1914.

EUROPEAN HARMONY: THE GREAT ILLUSION

French troops mount a charge during a battle in the Franco-Prussian War. The 1870–71 conflict profoundly changed the political landscape of Europe—and helped set the stage for World War I. Below left: Helmuth Carl Bernhard von Moltke (known as Moltke the Elder), chief of the Prussian General Staff, was the architect of Prussia's military victories over France and, earlier, Austria.

The political landscape of Europe, like other regions of the world, was shaped by war. But by the second decade of the 20th century, peace appeared to be taking root among Europe's major nations. By 1914, two generations had come of age since the last time any of the continent's *Great Powers* had clashed with one another on the battlefield. A sense of interdependence, and even an atmosphere of harmony, seemed to exist across

Europe's societies. Extensive commercial and financial ties among European countries helped boost industrial productivity and create increased wealth. Science and industry, flourishing in an era of peace and international cooperation, promised a new golden age of prosperity and progress.

Writers of the day gave voice to this optimism. One, the Englishman Norman Angell, declared in his 1910 book, *The Great Illusion*, that another European war was virtually impossible. So interdependent were Europe's countries that both the winners and the losers of such a conflict would suffer devastating economic harm. Thus, Angell reasoned, no country would dare start a war because doing so simply did not make sense. It was an idea that gained wide acceptance. *The Great Illusion* was quickly translated into 11 languages.

A DARKER REALITY

If war seemed almost unthinkable to Norman Angell and his many readers, a different, darker vision was contemplated by Friedrich von Bernhardi. A German general, Bernhardi wrote a book titled *Germany and the Next War*, which was published just a year after *The Great Illusion*. In his book, the general declared that enlarging its power is "the first and foremost duty of the State." And the way to fulfill that duty, he said, was through conquest.

While Bernhardi's book may not have reached nearly as wide an audience as did Angell's, his ideas were shared by an influential circle of military leaders, particularly in his native Germany. But even among European political and military leaders who did not agree with his view that a war was desirable, there were a number who considered a war inevitable. In spite of the surface appearance of harmony, Europe's Great Powers had for years been planning and preparing for war, building up their national armies and navies and developing ever more advanced weapons.

Of course, being prepared for war does not mean that war is inevitable. In fact, military preparedness may make war less likely. For by maintaining strong and ready armed forces, a country can deter neighbors who might otherwise contemplate aggressive action. And when a *balance of power* exists among individual nations or among rival alliances—that is, when potential adversaries are roughly equal in strength—stability often results. Because no side is assured of victory, everyone has an incentive to solve conflicts by means other than war, and hence all sides feel more secure.

But stability depends not just on actual conditions. It also depends on nations' perceptions. And in the early years of the 20th century, the Great Powers of Europe all felt threatened to some degree. To make themselves more secure, they undertook huge military buildups. This didn't lead to security, however. On the contrary, it simply fueled an accelerating arms race. When one nation made its military stronger, others felt vulnerable and struggled to catch up.

If, as many historians believe, the arms race between the Great Powers was a cause of (or at least a contributing factor to) World War I, several important questions arise. How did Europe's major nations become so fearful of one another that they transformed the continent into a giant armed camp? Why did diplomacy fail to defuse the building tensions? When did the path that led Europe to catastrophe in the summer of 1914 actually begin? These questions are complex, and not everyone agrees on the answers. But many historians begin their discussion of World War I by examining another war that was fought more than 40 years earlier.

"BLOOD AND IRON"

In 1870, France went to war with Prussia, a northern German kingdom whose territory bordered the

Baltic Sea and whose capital was Berlin. The Franco-Prussian War would dramatically shift political boundaries on the European continent. It left France weakened and Germany on the rise. It also sowed seeds of continuing conflict, which would be harvested with such bitter results in 1914.

The Franco-Prussian War marked the final step in a strategy to unify Germany under Prussian leadership through "blood and iron." The mastermind of that strategy was one of Europe's most remarkable statesmen: Prince Otto von Bismarck. When he became prime minister of Prussia in 1862, the German-speaking states of Europe were loosely aligned with one another in the German Confederation. Established in 1815, it

As Prussia's prime minister, Prince Otto von Bismarck masterminded the unification of Germany through "blood and iron." Later, as Germany's longtime chancellor, he would consolidate his country's position through shrewd diplomacy, playing potential rivals against one another and avoiding direct challenges to the overseas empires of other European Great Powers.

consisted of 39 states—35 monarchies and 4 free cities. Austria was unquestionably the dominant state in the confederation, and that rankled Bismarck and many of his fellow Prussians.

In 1866, the Prussian prime minister—against the wishes of Wilhelm I, his king—provoked a conflict with Austria over the administration of Schleswig and Holstein, two territories Prussia had earlier taken in a war with Denmark. Joined by a handful of other major kingdoms in the German Confederation, Austria anticipated a decisive victory. Instead, Prussia quickly smashed its enemies in what became known as the Seven Weeks' War.

In the aftermath of the war, Prussia annexed Schleswig-Holstein, Hanover, Hesse, and a few smaller states. In addition, Bismarck replaced the German Confederation with the North German Confederation. This new union, headed by Prussia, included more than a dozen states.

Bismarck was surprisingly lenient with Austria. While he excluded it from the North German Confederation, he didn't force Austria to give up territory. Bismarck didn't want to weaken Austria too much because his future plans included it as an ally. Nevertheless, the Seven Weeks' War left Austria in a weak enough position that its emperor, Franz Joseph, had to make political concessions to the Magyar (Hungarian) minority in the eastern part of his realm. Thus, in 1867 the Dual Monarchy, or Austria-Hungary, came into being.

THE FRANCO-PRUSSIAN WAR

French leaders eyed these developments with alarm. Did Otto von Bismarck have further ambitions? The French were right to be concerned, for Bismarck did have further ambitions—and France was his next target.

From a modern perspective, the immediate cause of the 1870–71 war between France and Prussia seems trivial. In June 1870, the Spanish crown was offered to Prince Leopold, a member of a branch of the house of Hohenzollern, Prussia's ruling family. After strenuous French objections, Leopold declined. On July 13, however, Bismarck received a diplomatic cable describing a brief exchange between the French ambassador and King Wilhelm I over the matter. Bismarck edited the cable in a manner that falsely suggested Wilhelm had insulted the French ambassador and, indirectly, France. Then Bismarck released the cable, called the Ems dispatch, to the press.

Publication of the Ems dispatch had the effect Bismarck desired: the French were enraged. On July 19,

France declared war on Prussia. This, in turn, rallied support among the southern German states for the North German Confederation.

While both France and Prussia had been preparing for a war, the Prussian military machine—led by General Helmuth Carl Bernhard von Moltke—proved superior on the battlefield. By early August the Prussian army had pushed across the border of Alsace, a region in northeastern France. They handed the

This photograph shows a group of Prussian infantrymen at the Battle of Sedan, September 1, 1871. Prussia dealt France a humiliating defeat at Sedan, where some 100,000 French soldiers surrendered and Emperor Napoleon III was captured.

French a series of defeats and isolated a large contingent of the French army at the city of Metz. When Napoleon III, the French emperor, tried to rescue this contingent, the Prussians inflicted a devastating blow. On September 1, at the town of Sedan, 100,000 French troops surrendered. The emperor himself was taken prisoner.

Now the Prussians marched on Paris. After surrounding the French capital during the third week of September, the Prussians laid siege to the city. As the weeks passed, the situation inside Paris became desperate. With no supplies getting in, hunger and disease stalked the streets. Many people died. Finally, on January 28, 1871, Paris surrendered. That same day, France and Prussia signed an *armistice* to bring an end to the fighting.

A BITTER PEACE

It is difficult to overestimate the effects of the Franco-Prussian War on the European political landscape. By the conclusion of the war, Bismarck had realized his dream of unifying Germany. The *Deutches Reich*, or German Empire, was created, with Prussia's Wilhelm I as its kaiser (emperor) and Bismarck as *chancellor*. Over the next decades this rising nation would take its place beside Europe's Great Powers, and even challenge the others for supremacy. France, meanwhile, threw off its emperor and reestablished a democratic government (the Third Republic).

But perhaps the most lasting effect of the Franco-Prussian War was the legacy of hatred the defeated French felt for the Germans. The peace terms that Prussian leaders imposed on France in 1871 were indeed harsh. First, France had to cede the majority of its Alsace and Lorraine regions to Germany. These were important territories. Both had significant deposits of iron ore; Lorraine also had coal deposits and was a grain-growing area. Second, the peace treaty allowed the German army to occupy France until France had paid damages of 5 billion francs (about $1 billion). At the time, this was an enormous sum. German leaders believed the payments would destroy France's economy, eliminating France as a potential enemy for the foreseeable future. They were wrong. Through an amazing effort, France paid the damages in full within three years.

But the French didn't forget the 5 billion francs. They didn't forget Alsace-Lorraine. They didn't forget other humiliations, such as the German army's triumphal march down the Champs-Elysées, the famed Paris boulevard. Over the years, French animosity toward the Germans grew. And members of all levels

A view of Mulhausen, a town in Alsace-Lorraine. When this photo was taken, around the turn of the 20th century, Germany controlled Alsace-Lorraine—a source of continuing bitterness among the French.

of French society, from politicians to generals to ordinary citizens, thirsted for revenge. Perhaps Victor Hugo, the great French author who served as a senator in the Third Republic, best summed up France's refusal to accept the defeat of 1870–71. "France," Hugo said, "will have but one thought: to reconstitute her forces, gather her energy, nourish her sacred anger, raise her young generation to form an army of the whole people, to work without cease, to study the methods and skills of our enemies, to become again a great France, . . . the France of an idea with a sword. . . . Then she will take back Alsace-Lorraine."

Such passions helped pave the road to World War I.

RIVALS
FOR
POWER

This painting depicts an official visit to France, in 1901, by Czar Nicholas II of Russia. The aggressive foreign policy of Kaiser Wilhelm II (bottom left) played a major role in driving France and Russia into an alliance.

"The sun never sets on the British Empire." This popular saying accurately reflected the extent of Great Britain's colonies and other imperial holdings by the late 1800s. In the 19th century, particularly during the long reign of Queen Victoria (1837–1901), the British brought enormous new territories under their control. To Canada, Australia, and other holdings were added India, Burma, Hong Kong, and huge sections of Africa. By 1914, the British Empire covered about 25 percent of the earth's land surface. Its approximately 400 million subjects constituted about a quarter of the world's population at that time.

IMPERIALIST EUROPE

Of course, Britain wasn't Europe's only *imperialist* nation. During the 19th century, France established major colonies in Africa and Indochina (present-day Vietnam, Laos, and Cambodia); it also controlled French Guiana (in South America), as well as a number of islands. Even less-powerful European countries had colonial possessions. Portugal and Belgium, for example, ruled large colonies in Africa. The Dutch East Indies (present-day Indonesia) belonged to the Netherlands.

Germany, too, acquired some overseas possessions. These included German East Africa (what is today Tanzania), German South-West Africa (Namibia), and Kamerun (Cameroon), as well as several Pacific island groups. But considering its position as one of the strongest military and industrial powers in continental Europe, Germany's overseas empire was rather paltry. It's true that other European powers had a head start on Germany, which wasn't unified until 1871. Yet much of Africa (as well as Southeast Asia) was colonized in the last three decades of the century, and Germany got considerably less than would be expected. The main reason? Otto von Bismarck, the chancellor who guided German foreign policy for two decades, wasn't interested in overseas colonies.

Historians aren't entirely sure why Bismarck shunned imperialist expansion—or why he departed from that policy for a brief period in the 1880s. The other European powers considered colonies an important reflection of their national prestige. More important, colonies provided real economic benefits. They were sources of raw materials, agricultural products, or other valuable commodities, and they often served as markets for finished goods manufactured in the mother country.

Bismarck seems to have believed that competing for overseas colonies would dilute German strength in Europe. But there is evidence that his policy was based on other strategic considerations as well. Bismarck had not wanted Germany to take Alsace-Lorraine from France after the Franco-Prussian War. He apparently believed—correctly, as it turned out—that doing so would make France a lasting enemy of Germany. By allowing, and even encouraging, France to pursue colonial possessions, Bismarck hoped to deflect French hostility away from Germany. Then, too, if potential

By the early 20th century, Europe dominated the globe. The British Empire alone included about one-quarter of earth's land area. Germany's ambitions to enlarge its empire caused friction with Britain and France and were a major cause of World War I.

Empires in 1914

- Britain
- France
- Germany
- Russia
- Austria-Hungary
- Ottoman
- Under British protection or influence
- Capitals of the Empires

rivals of Germany came into conflict over their colonies, that suited the German chancellor just fine.

A SHIFT IN GERMAN FOREIGN POLICY

In 1888, Kaiser Wilhelm II ascended to the German throne. Two years later, he forced Bismarck, who had served as chancellor for almost 20 years, to resign. After that, Germany's foreign policy changed dramatically. The new kaiser wasn't content to see his country remain simply a continental power. He want-

ed an overseas empire like that of the British and French, which in his view would confirm Germany's status as a world leader.

Unfortunately, by the 1890s the race to colonize Africa was largely over. And elsewhere around the world, little desirable territory remained that the European powers could easily take. This meant that any German empire-building efforts would almost inevitably cause conflict with other European powers. Germany could enlarge its empire only by taking colonies from other imperialist countries.

During the late 1890s, Germany began to expand its navy. That expansion accelerated with the Naval Law of 1900, which committed a large portion of the German military budget to shipbuilding. Under the counsel of Admiral Alfred von Tirpitz, Germany's naval minister, Kaiser Wilhelm had decided to create a navy strong enough to challenge Britain's dominance of the seas. Without its naval superiority, Great Britain would have a difficult time holding together its far-flung empire.

British leaders understood the threat Germany's naval buildup posed to their empire. Britain responded to the German challenge with a massive shipbuilding program of its own. In 1906 the British floated the battleship *Dreadnought*. Its superiority to all other warships of the day forced Germany (and other countries) to try to build ships of a similar class. This helped fuel a naval arms race that raised anxiety on all sides, pushing Europe closer to war.

Anxiety had earlier been raised by the kaiser's rejection of another cornerstone of Bismarck's foreign policy. Bismarck had crafted the so-called Reinsurance Treaty with Russia. By the terms of the agreement, Russia promised to remain neutral toward Germany unless Germany attacked France. For its part, Germany pledged neutrality toward Russia unless Russia attacked Austria-Hungary. The Russian Reinsurance Treaty served Bismarck's goal of trying to maintain both Austria-Hungary and Russia as allies. That policy helped protect Germany from having to deal with an enemy to its west (France) as well as one to its east (Russia). It also increased the likelihood that Germany could manage potential conflict between Russia and Austria-Hungary in the Balkans. In 1890, however, Kaiser Wilhelm renounced the Reinsurance Treaty. This helped push Russia, which now seemed to have reason to fear Germany, into a military alliance

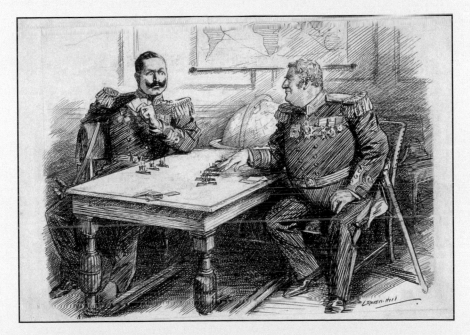

This cartoon, published in 1908 in the British humor magazine *Punch*, depicts a poker game between Kaiser Wilhelm and John Bull (a symbolic figure representing Great Britain). The two are betting not with money but with ships. The stakes were high in the naval race between Germany and Britain: without control of the seas, the British Empire would fall apart.

with France. In the years leading up to the outbreak of World War I, German military and political leaders worried constantly about being surrounded by enemies, but German policies had created that situation.

A TANGLE OF ALLIANCES

Fearful of their neighbors' intentions, all the Great Powers of Europe entered into alliances that committed them to go to war under certain circumstances. In theory, these alliances were defensive, and it was hoped that they would maintain a balance of power and thus prevent wars. But when Europe slid into crisis in the summer of 1914, the alliances did not stop the outbreak of World War I. If anything, they helped bring on the conflict.

Three of Europe's six Great Powers—Germany, Austria-Hungary, and Italy—were bound together as the Triple Alliance. By the terms of the pact, first signed in 1882, each member of the Triple Alliance pledged itself to fight in support of any other member that had been attacked by two other countries. The agreement was more important to the relatively weak Italy than to Germany or Austria-Hungary, which had concluded a dual alliance in 1879.

Counterbalancing the Triple Alliance, from the early 1890s on, were France and Russia. As recently as the 1850s, these two countries had been enemies in the Crimean War. But France hated and feared Germany, and Russia's emperor, Czar Alexander III, saw the need to find an ally after Kaiser Wilhelm jettisoned the Reinsurance Treaty. So France and Russia pledged to *mobilize* together if any member of the Triple Alliance mobilized against either of them. At the time, mobilization was widely understood to mean war.

In 1905, France's confidence in its alliance partner received a severe jolt. The previous year, hostilities had broken out between Russia and Japan over the two countries' competing ambitions in northeastern China. To the surprise of almost every international military expert of the time, Japan defeated the Russians decisively.

It's safe to assume that French military planners experienced many sleepless nights in the aftermath of the Russo-Japanese War. France's ally had been humiliated by a small country that, only five decades earlier, was almost completely isolated and had not even begun to industrialize. What help would Russia be in the event of a showdown with Germany?

In Russia, too, the military defeat (along with an unsuccessful revolution in January 1905) prompted some adjustments in thinking. Japan had undertaken a crash program of industrialization and military

In this woodcut print a huge hand, representing Japan's army, is about to seize Port Arthur, the site of one of the key campaigns in the 1904–05 Russo-Japanese War. Russia's surprising defeat by the Japanese had significant implications for the balance of power in Europe.

modernization in the last decades of the 19th century, and the results on the battlefield were convincing. Now Russia embarked on a similar program. France, for obvious reasons, helped finance the effort.

But what would happen if Germany attacked France before Russia had completed rearming and modernizing its forces? That question troubled leaders of another Great Power: Britain. Although the French were their longtime rivals, the British believed they couldn't afford to let France be overwhelmed by Germany. That would upset the European balance of power, and an emboldened Germany might threaten

British interests. Judging from the German naval buildup, the kaiser already had ambitions to challenge Britain. So in late 1905, British military officers began informal discussions with their French counterparts. These discussions grew out of a 1904 agreement known as the Entente Cordiale (French for "friendly understanding"). The Entente Cordiale wasn't an official defense treaty such as France had with Russia; public opinion in Britain wouldn't have stood for that. But over the years, Anglo-French military-to-military consultation helped lead to what the British statesman Winston Churchill referred to as a "veiled coalition." Leaders on both sides of the English Channel understood that Britain would lend assistance if France faced a threat that also might jeopardize British vital interests. In time the Anglo-French understanding evolved into the Triple Entente, an alliance between France, Britain, and Russia.

THE MOROCCO CRISES

Britain and France (and, by extension, Russia) were further pushed together by events in the North African country of Morocco. By the first years of the 20th century, France was preparing to incorporate Morocco into its empire. France already controlled two territories to the east of Morocco—Algeria (made

A secret handshake beneath the English Channel was the way one cartoonist depicted the 1904 Entente Cordiale. In the first years of the 20th century, British leaders avoided a formal, public alliance with France, but the Anglo-French understanding led to what Winston Churchill later called a "veiled coalition."

a part of France in 1881) and Tunisia (made a French *protectorate* in 1881). The European imperial powers basically accepted that Morocco fell within France's sphere of influence.

In 1905, however, Kaiser Wilhelm traveled to Morocco. There, in what was intended as a direct challenge to France, he proclaimed that Morocco should remain independent. The kaiser and his advisers, who were looking for a greater German role in Morocco, believed that France would be in no position to resist their demands. But Britain supported France, and a potential military confrontation was avoided only by the calling of an international conference to resolve the Morocco issue. In 1906, representatives of the countries attending the Algeciras Conference—Britain, France, Germany, Russia, Austria-Hungary, and a few others—signed a treaty that upheld France's leading role in Morocco. But the treaty also committed the European countries to respect Moroccan independence.

France had no intention of honoring that commitment, however. In 1911, a rebellion by desert tribes in the interior of Morocco provided the French with a convenient excuse for military involvement in the country. In May, French forces occupied the Moroccan capital of Fez.

Germany's foreign minister, Alfred von Kiderlen-Wächter, saw this as an opportunity for his country to make huge inroads in Africa. Kiderlen-Wächter would claim (with some justification) that France had violated the obligations it agreed to at the Algeciras Conference. And that, he would assert, rendered the treaty void. Germany would now demand that France give it vast territories in Africa as the price of Germany letting France proceed with its designs in Morocco. To drive home the point that Germany meant business, Kiderlen-Wächter dispatched a gunboat, the *Panther*, to the Moroccan port of Agadir. Remarkably, he was acting on his own: he had not even informed Germany's military leadership of his plan. On July 1, he announced Germany's demands in harsh terms that alarmed leaders in many European capitals. War seemed a distinct possibility.

The German foreign minister was gambling that the situation would not come to war, however. Britain, he believed, would be happy to see its imperial adversary France cut down a bit. Russia wouldn't risk war for French colonial ambitions. Thus, Kiderlen-Wächter reckoned, an isolated France would have no choice but to agree to Germany's demands. And in any event, Germany could count on Austria-Hungary and Italy, its Triple Alliance partners, to add weight to German demands.

Nearly all of these calculations turned out to be incorrect. Britain backed France, as did Russia. Meanwhile, Austria-Hungary refused to support Germany's demands, and Italy was noncommittal. After an extremely tense summer, Kaiser Wilhelm backed down, and the crisis passed.

But the incident had lasting effects, setting the stage for World War I. German leaders deeply resented the way Europe, in their view, had ganged up on Germany to prevent it from attaining the position it deserved. The Agadir crisis also increased German fears of being surrounded by hostile nations, especially because it exposed the weaknesses of the Triple Alliance. Italy simply couldn't be counted on as an ally, and Austria-Hungary would probably not fight with Germany unless its own interests were at stake. To address its newly apparent vulnerability, Germany undertook another huge arms buildup, this one concentrating on its land forces. Of course, other Great Powers felt threatened by the German buildup, so they responded in kind. This, in turn, simply heightened Germany's fears. Increasingly, German military leaders viewed a major European war as inevitable.

The second Morocco crisis led several key British leaders to the same conclusion. At an August 1911 meeting of Britain's Committee of Imperial Defence, it was decided that the Royal Navy as well as an army expeditionary force would be committed to fight with France in the event of a war with Germany.

The stage was now set for World War I. All that was required was for a spark to ignite the hostilities.

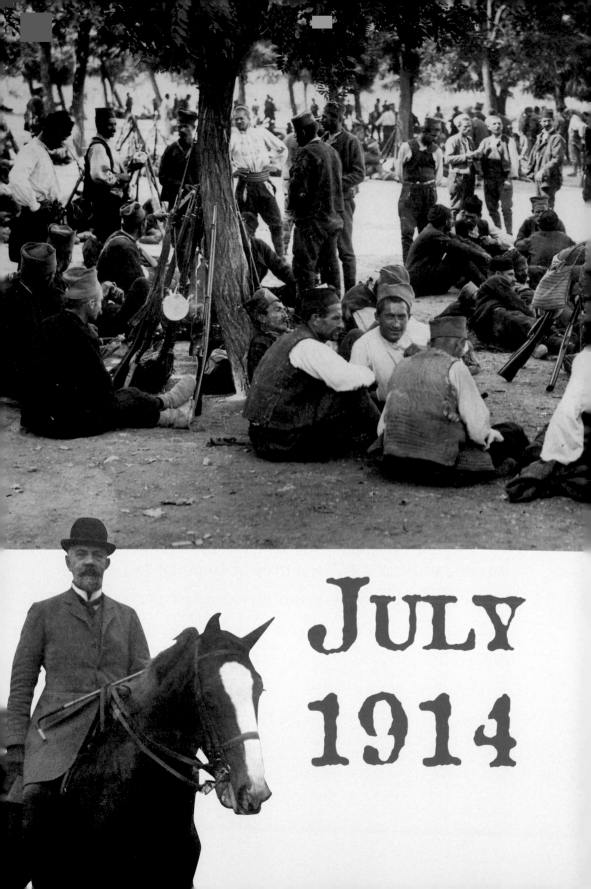

JULY 1914

Serbian soldiers encamped near Belgrade during the Second Balkan War. Serbia's territorial gains deeply troubled Austrian officials. After the assassination of Franz Ferdinand, German chancellor Theobald von Bethmann-Hollweg (bottom left) is believed to have formulated a plan by which Germany's ally Austria could dispose of the Serbian threat without risking a general European war.

The assassination of Archduke Franz Ferdinand and his wife, it has often been said, was the match that lit the fuse, causing all of Europe to explode in violence. Brigadier General S. L. A. Marshall chose another metaphor. "The crime," Marshall wrote in his book *World War I*, "was the small stone that, loosened, brings the avalanche." But perhaps both of these ways of looking at the conflict's beginnings are a bit misleading, for they suggest a certain inevitability. In reality, the archduke's assassination need not have led to World War I.

In Austria, the immediate reaction to the June 28 murders in Sarajevo was muted. Franz Ferdinand had not been well liked, and many Austrian officials—including his uncle the emperor—never really wanted him to inherit the throne. Initially there doesn't seem to have been any assumption that his assassination would touch off a war. Nor, at first, was there any call for war. In fact, some in the Austrian government considered the archduke's death a fortunate turn of events. "For me," Emperor Franz Joseph remarked, "it is a great worry less." In his diary, Count Leopold von Berchtold, the foreign minister of Austria-Hungary, said that there was "consternation and indignation, but also a certain easing of mood" at the first cabinet meeting after the Sarajevo killings.

Despite these relatively serene initial reactions, Austria-Hungary quickly set a course calculated to create a crisis. The ultimate goal was war with Serbia, which some officials in the Dual Monarchy viewed as the only way to reverse recent—and in their view, extremely alarming—developments in the Balkans. In fact, Berchtold had directed his Foreign Office to begin preparing a plan to destroy Serbia two weeks *before* the assassination of Franz Ferdinand. Why?

THE BALKAN WARS

In October of 1912, the countries of Montenegro, Serbia, Bulgaria, and Greece went to war with Ottoman Turkey. Russia—or at the very least, its minister to Serbia, Nicolai Hartwig—played a large role in encouraging this move. The once-mighty Ottoman Empire was clearly on its last legs, and it was already occupied by a war with Italy. Montenegro, Serbia, Bulgaria, and Greece saw an opportunity to expel the Ottomans completely from the Balkan Peninsula. Hartwig saw an opportunity to increase Russia's influence in the Balkans, and perhaps even unite the Balkans' Slavs under the leadership of Slavic Russia. The First Balkan War ended with a quick Ottoman defeat, and the Turks were forced out of Albania, Kosovo, and Macedonia.

But when Macedonia was divided among the victors, Bulgaria believed that it had received too little, and Serbia and Greece too much. In late June 1913, Bulgarian forces launched surprise attacks on these two former allies, touching off the Second Balkan War. Within about a month, however, Bulgaria had been defeated by Serbia and Greece, which were joined by Romania and Turkey.

When the Balkan Wars had ended, Serbia controlled Kosovo and Macedonia. In just one year's

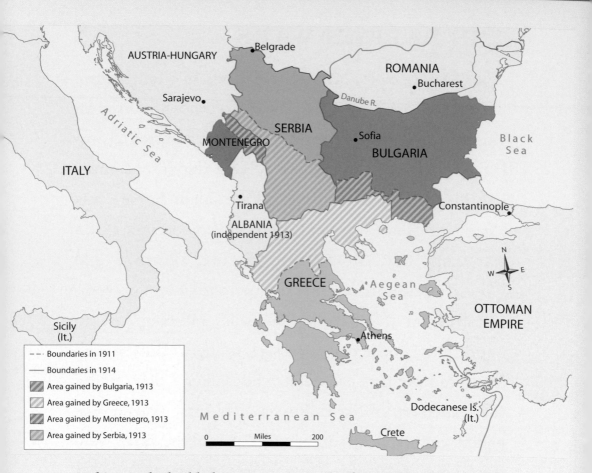

AUSTRIA-HUNGARY

Belgrade

ROMANIA

Bucharest

Sarajevo

Danube R.

SERBIA

Sofia

MONTENEGRO

BULGARIA

Black Sea

ITALY

Adriatic Sea

Tirana

Constantinople

ALBANIA
(independent 1913)

GREECE

Aegean
Sea

OTTOMAN
EMPIRE

Sicily
(It.)

Athens

Dodecanese Is.
(It.)

Mediterranean Sea

Crete

- - - Boundaries in 1911
——— Boundaries in 1914
▨ Area gained by Bulgaria, 1913
▨ Area gained by Greece, 1913
▨ Area gained by Montenegro, 1913
▨ Area gained by Serbia, 1913

0   Miles   200

Serbia nearly doubled its size as a result of the Balkan Wars—and, Austrian officials worried, Serbian territorial ambitions were still not satisfied.

time, Serbia had roughly doubled its territory.

In Vienna, officials of the Dual Monarchy saw in the Serbian expansion a mortal threat. They knew Serbia had designs on Bosnia and Herzegovina. They worried that Serbia would stir up further unrest among Austria-Hungary's large, and already restless, Slavic population. And they saw the hand of Russia behind the entire Balkan mess. In this analysis, the

Austro-Hungarian officials were pretty much on the mark. Russia's foreign minister had earlier told the Serbian ambassador to his country, "We shall shake Austria to the foundations." He also said that Serbia should consider the territorial gains it made as the result of the Balkan Wars "as an installment, for the future belongs to us."

A "BLANK CHECK" GOES UNCASHED

The assassinations of Franz Ferdinand and Sophie, in the opinion of Austrian officials such as Foreign Minister Berchtold, could provide a justification for disposing of the Serbian threat. Two of the conspirators—the bomb-thrower Cabrinovic and the shooter and actual killer Princip—had been captured at the scene of the crime. In the days that followed, four other plotters were rounded up. While they were all citizens of Bosnia-Herzegovina—and hence Austro-Hungarian, rather than Serbian,

Foreign Minister Leopold von Berchtold believed that Slavic nationalism, fomented largely by Serbia, threatened the very survival of Austria-Hungary. Two weeks before the murders of Franz Ferdinand and Sophie in Sarajevo, he directed his subordinates to develop a plan to destroy Serbia.

subjects—they were Serb nationalists. And an Austrian investigation indicated that a major in the Serbian army had supplied the assassins' pistols and bombs. Still, as an Austrian sent from Vienna to look into the matter informed his superiors, "There is nothing to indicate that the Serbian Government knew about the plot."

But the absence of proof that the Serbian government was involved in the crime wasn't the biggest barrier to Austria-Hungary's plans to attack Serbia. The biggest barrier was Russia. If Russia threw its military muscle behind its ally Serbia, Austria-Hungary faced certain defeat on the battlefield. What Austria-Hungary needed was Germany's assurance that it would join the fight if Russia (and perhaps France) intervened.

On July 5, 1914, Kaiser Wilhelm secretly gave Austria-Hungary that assurance. The kaiser had been furious at the Sarajevo killings. Not only had he counted Franz Ferdinand as a friend, but for obvious reasons he didn't like to see monarchs assassinated. He was also somewhat of an anti-Slav bigot. "The Serbs," he remarked, "must be disposed of and that right soon!"

On July 6, Germany's military and political leaders endorsed the kaiser's guarantee, giving Austria-Hungary a "blank check" to deal with Serbia. A plan of action was formulated. Its author is believed to have been Germany's chancellor, Theobald von Beth-mann-Hollweg. The plan envisioned Austria-Hungary striking quickly and crushing Serbia before Russia, France, or Britain had time to react. With the deed accomplished—and with no reason to suspect that Austria-Hungary had not acted in retribution for the assassination of the archduke—the Great Powers would accept the outcome, Bethmann-Hollweg believed.

To avoid alerting the rest of Europe that something extraordinary might be in the works, and to make it appear that Germany had no role in Austria-Hungary's invasion of Serbia, top German military and political officials went on their summer vacations as usual. On July 6, Kaiser Wilhelm boarded the royal yacht for his annual cruise. At most, he reckoned, three weeks would pass before Austria-Hungary had brought Serbia to its knees. He would still be at sea.

Little did the kaiser know, Chancellor Bethmann-Hollweg's plan would run into trouble almost immediately. Austria's foreign minister, Count Berchtold, supported the plan enthusiastically. But on July 7, when the Dual Monarchy's cabinet met to discuss the plan, opposition was voiced by Hungary's prime minister, Count István Tisza—and because of the way the Dual Monarchy was structured politically, his approval was needed. Tisza doubted that Russia would stand for an invasion of Serbia, and Russian intervention might trigger a world war. After much debate, it was agreed that Austria-Hungary would issue an **ultimatum** to Serbia. War would follow only if the Serbian government didn't accept the conditions. While Berchtold intended to make sure the ultimatum was almost impossible for Serbia to accept, it was now July 14. A full week had been lost in the cabinet deliberations.

Meanwhile, Field Marshal Franz Conrad von Hötzendorf, the army chief of staff, informed Berchtold that leaves of absence issued to Austrian soldiers so that they could go home to help in the

The opposition of Count István Tisza, the prime minister of Hungary, helped scuttle the initial plan to strike Serbia quickly, before Russia, Britain, or France could react. Tisza insisted that Austria-Hungary present Serbia with an ultimatum.

harvest would not expire until July 25. Ordering the soldiers to report to their units before then would give away Austria-Hungary's hostile plans. In addition, Berchtold knew that President Raymond Poincaré and Prime Minister René Viviani of France were scheduled to visit Russia around that time, and he didn't want to give France and Russia the opportunity to coordinate their response. So there was no way Austria-Hungary would be in a position to invade Serbia until the last week of July at the earliest.

By July 16, hints of what Austria-Hungary intended to do had begun to leak out. While there was as yet no widespread sense that a crisis loomed, foreign ministry officials in the capitals of Europe began paying more attention to the situation. Clearly the plan for a lightning strike against Serbia that would catch the Great Powers by surprise was no longer feasible. On the 19th, Gottlieb von Jagow, Germany's foreign minister, introduced a revised strategy: "localization" of the conflict. If war came, Jagow informed his counterparts throughout Europe, the matter should remain between Austria-Hungary and Serbia. The Great Powers had no reason to get involved, he said. At the same time, Jagow falsely insisted that Germany had no knowledge of the Dual Monarchy's plans or what demands it might make on Serbia.

THE ULTIMATUM

Austria-Hungary finally delivered its ultimatum to Serbia at 6 P.M. on July 23. A reply was demanded within 48 hours.

When they read the ultimatum, Europe's foreign ministers and diplomats were amazed at its harshness. Most doubted that Serbia would accept Austria-Hungary's humiliating terms. A flurry of diplomatic activity ensued to head off the looming conflict. Sir Edward Grey, Britain's foreign secretary, asked Germany to use its influence with Austria-Hungary to get the 48-hour deadline for Serbia's response extended. At the same time, Grey proposed that Germany, Britain, France, and Italy act together to mediate the conflict. Russian officials also advocated the postponement of the deadline, even making direct requests to Berchtold, but they were rebuffed.

In Belgrade, the capital of Serbia, Serbian ministers were in the midst of extremely tense discussions about how to reply to the ultimatum. After much back and forth, they decided to accept almost all of Austria-Hungary's demands. On the evening of July 25, Nicola Pasic, the Serbian prime minister, rushed his government's response to the Austrian minister in Belgrade. He arrived right around the six o'clock deadline. Glancing briefly at the document, the

Historians are unsure what, if anything, Serbia's prime minister, Nicola Pasic, knew about the plot to assassinate Franz Ferdinand. But the Black Hand long opposed the moderate Pasic, who unsuccessfully tried to avert war with Austria-Hungary in late July 1914 by agreeing to most of the terms of the Austrian ultimatum.

Austrian minister proceeded to officially break off diplomatic relations, as he had been instructed.

But Austria did not immediately attack Serbia, or even declare war. So it seemed that there was still a chance to avert conflict. On July 26, Sir Arthur Nicholson, head of the British Foreign Office, formulated a diplomatic initiative that won the support of Foreign Secretary Grey. The German, French, and Italian ambassadors in London were invited to join a conference with British officials to defuse the crisis. Germany officially rejected the proposal, but Kaiser Wilhelm had not yet returned from his summer cruise.

On July 28, the day after his return to Germany, the kaiser saw the Serbian reply to Austria-Hungary's

ultimatum for the first time. He considered it "a capit-
ulation of the most humiliating kind" and believed that
"every cause for war has vanished." Wilhelm thought
that a "halt in Belgrade" formula could prevent the conflict between Austria-Hungary and Serbia from developing into a larger European war. Under such a plan,
the Austrian army would occupy Serbia's capital while
peace terms were worked out. Wilhelm offered to per-
sonally mediate for peace, and he instructed Foreign
Minister Jagow to convey that message to officials in
Vienna. Jagow did not pass the message along. Nor
would other German officials heed the kaiser's judg-
ment that there was no longer any reason for war.
Unbeknownst to Wilhelm, important decisions had
been made while he was still on his summer cruise.

One group that appears to have taken a lead in
making some momentous decisions is Germany's
General Staff. Particularly influential in the unfolding
events was its chief, General Helmuth Johannes Ludwig von Moltke—the nephew and namesake of the leg-
endary Prussian general who defeated Austria and
then France in the wars that led to German unification. Moltke the Younger, as he was called, had
thought for some time that a war with Russia and
France was inevitable, and that the sooner it was
fought, the better Germany's chances of winning. With

each passing year, he believed, Russia was getting stronger, and by 1917 it would be in a position to overwhelm Germany. Earlier in 1914, in fact, Moltke had asked Jagow to find a pretext by which a *preventive war* could be launched. As the first weeks of July passed with no attack on Serbia by Austria-Hungary, Moltke appears to have seen an opportunity for his war. But to ensure the support of the German people, he regarded it as essential that Russia or France be seen as the aggressor.

THE FIRST WAR DECLARATION

On July 28, Austria-Hungary finally declared war on Serbia. But aside from a brief Austrian artillery barrage against Belgrade, no fighting followed, and it still appeared that a general European war might be avoided. Sir Edward Grey, the British foreign secretary, continued to float proposals for negotiations. Grey understood what was at stake. "If war breaks out," he predicted, "it will be the greatest catastrophe that the world has ever seen."

Kaiser Wilhelm and his cousin Nicholas II, the czar of Russia, also sought to contain the conflict between Austria-Hungary and Serbia. The two exchanged a series of cables asking for each other's support in averting a wider war. "An ignoble war has

Unser Kaiser an sein Volk

„Eine schwere Stunde ist heute über Deutschland hereingebrochen. Neider überall zwingen uns zu gerechter Verteidigung. Man drückt uns das Schwert in die Hand. Ich hoffe, daß wir, wenn es nicht in letzter Stunde meinen Bemühungen gelingt, die Gegner zum Einsehen zu bringen und den Frieden zu erhalten, das Schwert mit Gottes Hilfe so führen werden, daß wir es mit Ehren wieder in die Scheide stecken können. Enorme Opfer an Gut und Blut würde ein Krieg vom deutschen Volke fordern, den Gegnern aber würden wir zeigen, was es heißt, Deutschland anzugreifen. Und nun empfehle ich Euch Gott. Jetzt geht in die Kirche, kniet nieder vor Gott und bittet ihn um Hilfe für unser braves Heer!"

Berlin, 31. Juli 1914.

The text of this German poster is a proclamation by Kaiser Wilhelm preparing his people for war. It was issued on July 31, 1914, following Russian mobilization. Earlier, hoping to prevent Austria-Hungary's conflict with Serbia from developing into a larger European war, the kaiser had advocated the "halt in Belgrade" formula.

been declared on a weak country. . . . To try and avoid such a calamity as a European war, I beg you in the name of our old friendship to do what you can to stop your allies from going too far," Nicholas wrote.

"I am exerting my utmost influence to induce the Austrians to deal straightly," Wilhelm insisted. (He was still unaware that his generals and foreign minister were undermining his peace efforts.)

Upon returning from Russia, President Raymond Poincaré and Prime Minister René Viviani ordered all French soldiers to withdraw six miles from the frontier with Germany to avoid any provocation.

Nevertheless, the situation deteriorated. On July 30, Russia began a mobilization of troops as a precautionary measure. This was the pretext Helmuth von Moltke was hoping for: it would allow him to paint Germany as being threatened by its enemies. Germany issued an ultimatum demanding that Russia call off its mobilization by noon on August 1, or Germany would mobilize against Russia—and that would mean a war. Germany also issued an ultimatum to France threatening war unless France agreed to remain neutral in any Russo-German conflict.

THE
GREAT
WAR

A dead German soldier behind his machine gun. Inset: Detail from a British recruiting poster putting out the call for more troops. On the battlefields of World War I, traditional tactics such as the massed infantry charge ran up against modern weapons like machine guns and poison gas. The result was carnage on a scale never before imagined.

O n August 1, 1914, Germany declared war on Russia, which had failed to respond to the ultimatum to cease its mobilization. That same day, Germany invaded Luxembourg. This was a necessary first step in Moltke's war plans—plans that were so secret, the details were not even known to Kaiser Wilhelm or Chancellor Bethmann-Hollweg. Essentially following the so-called Schlieffen Plan, developed by his predecessor,

Moltke would launch a huge invasion force at France by way of Luxembourg and Belgium. While a small number of German units—joined by the armies of Austria-Hungary—fought a holding action against Russia in the east, the bulk of the German army would sweep across northern France, wheel toward Paris, and completely destroy the French forces within six weeks. Then these troops would be moved to the eastern front to knock out Russia.

THE WAR IS JOINED

On August 3, Germany declared war on France, falsely alleging that French forces had bombed the German city of Nuremberg. Despite Britain's informal military understanding with France, some Liberal Party members of the British Parliament opposed entering the war. But when German troops invaded Belgium, a country whose neutrality Britain was obligated by treaty to uphold, the objections of the antiwar group evaporated. At midnight on August 4, Great Britain declared war on Germany. World War I—known at the time as the Great War—had begun.

Throughout August, it appeared that Moltke's plan for a quick victory in the west might succeed, as the German armies steadily advanced. But in September, the French launched a successful counterattack at the

Battle of the Marne. Afterward, both sides dug in, and soon trenches extended from the French border with Switzerland in the south to Flanders in Belgium to the north. Over the next three and a half years, infantry attacks and counterattacks against entrenched positions—which were defended by machine guns and barbed wire—claimed hundreds of thousands of lives, yet the western front barely moved. This was mass slaughter of a kind never before seen.

But the fighting wasn't confined to France and Belgium. The Great War truly was a world war. Bloody battles were fought in eastern, southern, and southeastern Europe; in the African colonies; in the Middle East; and in Asia. And a host of countries became involved in the war. Among those that eventually joined the coalition led by Germany and Austria-Hungary, known as the Central Powers, were the Ottoman Empire and Bulgaria. The Allies, led by France, Great Britain, and Russia, were joined by more than 20 nations, including Italy and, in 1917, the United States. It was the U.S. entry into the conflict that broke the stalemate, tipping the balance in favor of the Allies. On November 11, 1918, defeated Germany agreed to an armistice, and the guns finally fell silent. The Great War had claimed the lives of approximately 20 million soldiers and civilians. An additional 21 million servicemen had been wounded.

On May 7, 1915, a German submarine torpedoed and sank the ocean liner *Lusitania* off the coast of Ireland. The attack, which claimed the lives of nearly 1,200 passengers and crew, served as a rallying cry for the British. It also helped turn American public opinion against Germany, and two years later the United States entered the war on the side of the Allies.

AFTERMATH

At the outset of the war, General Helmuth von Moltke had written that Europe was embarking on "the struggle that will decide the course of history for the next hundred years." In ways that he couldn't possibly foresee, he was right. For example, heavy losses suffered by the Russian army helped inspire a revolution that overthrew the czar in 1917 and eventually led to the creation of the Soviet Union. That Communist country would dominate Eastern Europe and oppose the U.S.-led West in the ideological struggle known as the Cold War, which defined world politics from the late 1940s to the early 1990s. British and French actions in the Middle East during and after World War I helped set the stage for the still-unresolved Arab-Israeli conflict. But most significantly, the harsh peace terms that the victorious Allies imposed on defeated Germany in the 1919 Treaty of Versailles would lead, only a generation later, to World War II.

The shots fired by Gavrilo Princip on that long-ago June morning in 1914 reverberate to this day.

The leaders of the major victorious nations, the so-called Big Four (from left: David Lloyd George of Great Britain, Vittorio Orlando of Italy, Georges Clemenceau of France, and Woodrow Wilson of the United States), chat during a break in the Paris peace talks, 1919. The harsh terms the Versailles Treaty imposed on defeated Germany would lead to World War II just 20 years later.

1866 Prussia defeats Austria in the Seven Weeks' War, forms the North German Confederation.

1870–71 Prussia defeats France in the Franco-Prussian War, forces France to cede Alsace-Lorraine; the German Empire is formed.

1878 The Congress of Berlin recognizes Serbia as an independent state; the Ottoman Empire retains control of Bosnia and Herzegovina in name, but Austria-Hungary is given actual administrative control.

1879 Germany and Austria-Hungary form a defensive alliance.

1882 The Triple Alliance is formed between Germany, Austria-Hungary, and Italy.

1888 Wilhelm II becomes Germany's kaiser.

1890 Kaiser Wilhelm forces Otto von Bismarck to resign from his post as chancellor, renounces the Reinsurance Treaty with Russia.

1900 The German Naval Law touches off a military shipbuilding race, particularly with Great Britain.

1904 Britain and France agree to the Entente Cordiale, paving the way for closer relations.

1905 Russia is defeated by Japan in the Russo-Japanese War; Kaiser Wilhelm precipitates the first Morocco crisis; British and French military officials begin informal discussions.

1908 Taking advantage of confusion in Ottoman Turkey caused by the Young Turk uprising, Austria-Hungary annexes Bosnia and Herzegovina; the ultranationalist Serb organization called the Black Hand (also known as "Union or Death") is formed.

1911 After French military forces intervene in Morocco, the German foreign minister Alfred von Kiderlen-Wächter dispatches the gunboat *Panther* to Agadir, precipitating the second Morocco crisis.

1912   Montenegro, Serbia, Bulgaria, and Greece defeat Ottoman Turkey in the First Balkan War.

1913   Serbia and Greece, joined by Romania and Turkey, defeat Bulgaria in the Second Balkan War; as a result, Serbia greatly enlarges its territory.

1914   JUNE 28: Archduke Franz Ferdinand, heir to the throne of Austria-Hungary, is assassinated by a Bosnian Serb nationalist in Sarajevo.

JULY 5–6: Kaiser Wilhelm and the German government give Austria-Hungary a "blank check" to punish Serbia.

JULY 23: Austria-Hungary issues an ultimatum to Serbia.

JULY 25: Austria-Hungary rejects the Serbian reply, breaks off diplomatic relations.

JULY 28: Austria-Hungary declares war on Serbia.

AUGUST 1: Germany declares war on Russia.

AUGUST 3: Germany declares war on France.

AUGUST 4: Following Germany's invasion of Belgium, Great Britain declares war on Germany.

ANNEX—to incorporate a territory or country within a larger state.

ARMISTICE—an agreement to suspend hostilities; truce.

BALANCE OF POWER—parity between the armed forces of rival nations or coalitions.

BALKANS—the mountainous peninsula in southeastern Europe that includes, among other countries, Greece, Serbia, Montenegro, Croatia, and Bulgaria.

CHANCELLOR—in the German Empire, the kaiser's chief minister.

GREAT POWERS—the most important states of Europe during the period leading up to World War I; considered to include Great Britain, France, Germany, Italy, Austria-Hungary, and Russia.

HEIR—a person who is in line to succeed a hereditary ruler such as an emperor or king.

IMPERIALIST—concerning or characteristic of imperialism, a policy by which a nation seeks to extend its power by directly acquiring new territory or by exercising indirect control over other lands and peoples.

MOBILIZE—to call up or assemble armed forces in preparation for war.

NATIONALISM—loyalty to one's own ethnic group or people, which often finds expression in a desire for an independent state.

PREVENTIVE WAR—a war undertaken not in self-defense but to forestall the possibility of a future threat.

PROTECTORATE—a relatively weak territory or country to which a stronger nation extends protection and, typically, over which it exercises a degree of control.

SLAVS—any of a group of peoples speaking a Slavic language, such as the Russians and the Serbs.

ULTIMATUM—a demand or set of demands issued by one state to another, the refusal to comply with which is considered a cause for further action such as war.

BOOKS FOR STUDENTS:

Bernard, Catherine. *The British Empire and Queen Victoria in World History*. Berkeley Heights, N.J.: Enslow, 2003.

Hatt, Christine. *World War I, 1914–1918*. New York: Franklin Watts, 2001.

Malam, John. *World War I: Armistice Day*. North Mankato, Minn.: Smart Apple Media, 2003.

Rice, Earle. *The First Battle of the Marne*. Philadelphia: Chelsea House, 2002.

BOOKS FOR OLDER READERS:

Fromkin, David. *Europe's Last Summer: Who Started the Great War in 1914?* New York: Alfred A. Knopf, 2004.

Keegan, John. *The First World War*. New York: Vintage Books, 2000.

Marshall, S. L. A. *World War I*. New York and Boston: Houghton Mifflin, 2001.

Tuchman, Barbara W. *The Guns of August*. New York: Ballantine Books, 1994.

INTERNET RESOURCES

HTTP://WWW.FIRSTWORLDWAR.COM/

This website offers a multifaceted view of the Great War, with essays on leaders, causes, weapons, and major battles, along with pictures and maps.

HTTP://WWW.PBS.ORG/GREATWAR/

Companion website for the PBS program "The Great War and the Shaping of the 20th Century."

HTTP://NEWS.BBC.CO.UK/1/HI/SPECIAL_REPORT/1998/10/98/WORLD_WAR_I/197437.STM

This British Broadcasting Corporation website, developed for the 80th anniversary of the end of World War I, contains historical analysis, accounts of major battles, photos and newsreel footage, archived radio interviews, and letters from soldiers.

HTTP://WWW.GREATWARDIFFERENT.COM/GREAT_WAR/

Making ample use of eyewitness accounts, news stories, and period photographs, this website provides intriguing looks at a variety of World War I–related topics.

Alexander III, czar of Russia, 37
Algeciras Conference of 1906, 41
Alsace-Lorraine, 24, 26, 27, 31
Austria-Hungary, *9*, 13, 14, 22, 23,
    34–36, 41–43, 46–55, 57, 58, 62, 63
    ethnic groups in, 11, 12, 14, 23

Balkan Peninsula, 12, 13, 46, 47, 48, 49
Balkan wars, 47, *48*, 49
Belgium, 62, 63
Berchtold, Leopold von, 46, *49*, 51, 52,
    53, 54
Bethmann-Hollweg, Theobald von, *44*,
    51, 61
Bismarck, Otto von, *21*, 22, 23, 25, 31,
    32, 34–35
Black Hand, 14
Bosnia-Herzegovina, 11–14, 48, 49
Bulgaria, 47, 63

Cabrinovic, Nedjelko, 14, 49
Congress of Berlin, 13
Conrad von Hötzendorf, Franz, 52
Crimean War, 37

Ems dispatch, 23–24
Entente Cordiale, 39

France, 20, 21, 23–26, *29*, 30, 31,
    33–43, 50–55, 56–59, 62–65
Franco-Prussian War, *16–17*, 20–21,
    23–27, 31
Franz Ferdinand, *9*, 10–12, 14, 15,
    45–46, 49, 50
Franz Joseph, emperor of Austria-
    Hungary, 10, 11, 23, 46

Germany, 18, 19, 21, 25, 30, 32–38,
    41–43, 50, 51, 53–55, 57, 59, 61–65
Great Britain, 29–30, 33, 34, *35*, 39,
    41–43, 51, 54, 62–65
Greece, 47
Grey, Edward, 54, 55, 57

Hartwig, Nicolai, 47
Hungary, 13

Italy, 36, 42, 43, 47, 54, 55, 63

Jagow, Gottlieb von, 53, 56
Japan, 37–38

Kiderlen-Wächter, Alfred von, 41, 42

Luxembourg, 61, 62

Magyars, 11, 23
Moltke, Helmuth Carl Bernhard von (the
    Elder), *16*, 24
Moltke, Helmuth Johannes Ludwig von
    (the Younger), 56, 59, 61, 62, 64
Montenegro, 13, 47
Morocco crisis, 39–43

Napoleon III, emperor of France, 25
Naval Law of 1900, 34
Nicholas II, czar of Russia, *28*, 57
Nicholson, Arthur, 55

Ottoman Empire, 12–13, 47, 63

Pasic, Nicola, 54, *55*
Poincaré, Raymond, 53, 59
Princip, Gavrilo, *8*, 15, 49, 65
Prussia, 20–21, 22, 23, 24, 25

Reinsurance Treaty, 34–35
Russia, 12, 13, 34, 35, 37–39, 41, 42, 47,
    48, 50–54, 56–59, 61–65
Russo-Japanese War, 37, 38

Sarajevo, *9*, 12, 14, 15, 46, 50
Serbia, 13, 46–55, 57, 58
Seven Weeks' War, 22
Sophie (wife of Franz Ferdinand), *9*,
    11–12, 15, 45, 49

Treaty of Versailles, 65
Tirpitz, Alfred von, 34
Tisza, István, 51, *52*
Triple Alliance, 36, 37, 42–43
Triple Entente, 39

United States, 63

Victoria, queen of England, 29
Vienna, 11, 13, 14, 48
Viviani, René, 53, 59

Wilhelm I, emperor of Germany, 22, 23,
    25
Wilhelm II, emperor of Germany, *28*,
    32–33, 34, *35*, 37, 39, 40, 42, 50, 51,
    55, 56, 57, *58*, 59, 61
World War I, 15, 20, 27, 36, 42, 61–65

Numbers in **bold italics** refer to captions.

PICTURE CREDITS

ABOUT THE AUTHOR

JOHN ZIFF, an editor with more than 20 years of experience in publishing, occasionally writes books for young adults. He lives outside Philadelphia with his wife, Clare, and children, Jane and Peter.